RODERICK WATSON was born and edu
ated in 1965 and taught at the Uni.
before going to Cambridge to do research on the poe...,
MacDiarmid. His books include *Hugh MacDiarmid, The Literature of Scotland, The Poetry of Scotland* and (with Martin Gray) *The Penguin Book of the Bicycle*. He teaches at the University of Stirling where he specialises in Scottish literature and has written and lectured widely in this field.

Roderick Watson was awarded a Scottish Arts Council Writer's Bursary and was one of the 'Heretics' performers in Edinburgh in the 1970s. Previous collections include *Trio* (New York, 1971) and *True History on the Walls* (Edinburgh, 1977) and his poetry has since appeared in numerous magazines and many anthologies. He has read his own work in Scotland and Europe and works with creative writing classes, schools and writers' groups. His other interests include cycling, motorcycling and modern jazz.

Into the Blue Wavelengths

Love poems and elegies

RODERICK WATSON

Luath Press Limited

EDINBURGH

www.luath.co.uk

First Published 2004

The author's right to be identified as author of this book under the
Copyright, Designer and Patents Acts 1988 has been asserted.

The publisher acknowledges subsidy from

 Scottish **Arts** Council

towards the publication of this book.

The paper used in this book is recyclable. It is made from low
chlorine pulps produced in a low energy, low emission manner
from renewable forests.

Printed and bound by
DigiSource (GB), Livingston

Typeset in Sabon 10.5 by
S Fairgrieve, Edinburgh 0131 658 1763

for
Celia, Joanna, Christopher
. . . here we all were . . .

Acknowledgements

Acknowledgements are due to the following publications in which some of these poems first appeared: *Akros, Aquarius, Cencrastus, Chapman, Clanjamfrie, Hairst, Lines Review, The Literary Review, Mica, Orbis, The Scottish Review, The Scotsman, Verse*; also the following anthologies: *Akros Verse 1965-82, Birds, Not Just Another Pile of Bricks, Twenty of the Best, Under Cover, Full Strength Angels, Scottish Literature in the Twentieth Century*; also BBC Radio Scotland, BBC Radio 3, STV.

My thanks go also to the Scottish Arts Council for their support of this volume.

*Perhaps all poems are love poems –
and elegies as well*

Contents

Into the blue . . .   13

Baby Dancer   15
Transparencies   16
The Photographer Memory   17
Out of Ward 6   19
Family Group   21
MacDiarmid at the End of the World   23
In the Fall Woods   24
Surface Tensions   25
Sycamore Leaf for Celia   27
Londonderry Love Poem: Certainties   28
Reflexions   29
Poem   30
Short Stories
    1. *Eve*   31
    2. *Dido*   32
    3. *Troilus*   33
On the Sea Rim   35

Reflections . . .   37

Mirrored   39
The Daily Life of Statues   40
Trahison des Poètes   42
All the Time   43
A Chinese Moment by the Duckpond   44
Sunday Morning Evolution Lesson Poem   46

Postcards Home
    1. *Postcards*   48
    2. *The Crab in Springtime*   50
    3. *Looking through the Glass*   51
    4. *Brown Study*   52
    5. *Holiday Cottage*   53
    6. *From the Compartment*   54
    7. *Back in the Room Now*   55
Lines for Scotland   56

Wavelengths . . .   57

Bla Bheinn   59
Skye Shore   60
Nature Study   62
Photocopy   63
FM   64
Wavelengths   65
Shades
    1. *Hugh MacDiarmid*   68
    2. *Sydney Goodsir Smith*   69
    3. *Robert Garioch*   70
Winding the Clock   71
The Slope   73
The Schools of Siena
    1. *Crossing to Tuscany*   75
    2. *Towards the Sun*   77
    3. *No. 1 Via d'Ingresso*   78
    4. *The Life*   79
Beyond the Edge   80
Slender Walker   82
End-notes and echoes   84

Into the Blue . . .

Baby Dancer

My daughter dances
barefoot on the living room floor
Bone on bone on bone
on bone on bone on stone
on stone. She raises her fist
she raises her fists for joy:

Oh!   You old   old   world!

Transparencies

Caught one more time   right
at a thousandth of a second
we turn from the picnic   playing
the fool: for old shoeboxes and

fat yellow packets of babies   skies
back gardens   friends on the beach
things cut off at the edges
and gone relatives in celluloid
with ginger faces   green hair.

       (It is the past   that touches
       where we cannot   reach
       and tells what we cannot   help
       whose witness is deployed
       already   around our shaded eyes.)

And there I stand deep in the dead
grass on a lion-coloured slope
hungry for more   holding
a glass and my daughter up to the light;

greeting   the waves passing through
bathing   at the bottom of the sun's well
until   in a moment   we burn out
and disappear   (hill grass child man)
into the blizzard . . . whiteness . . . void

The Photographer Memory

It comes when you don't expect it until you're looking years
    later
at an iron railing broken and set with wire   or a girl's ears
that turn-in at the tip into her hair   I recognise them
– things at the edge that weren't there when the picture was
    taken.
Or do they develop afterwards   very slowly   rising into
a light that was never quite forsaken?

    – Where I met you
at the beach on the hot verge of a twisted pinewood   walking
out of the blinding Tuscan glare with something held in your
    hand.
Under an umbrella along the way a family sits with the ghosts
of children   baskets   bottles of wine and acqua minerale
– a good time – fading all around them; and an ancient lady
spreads her chestnut belly in horizontal bikini folds
thick with suncream above her thighs   to eat a lump of bread
and olive oil. The feast at hand. Her upper groin is a peach
of dark whiskers where delicately and severally arrested stand
    crumbs
of nutritious crust   rippling as she chews.   Salty pearls
roll sideways across her skin.   Her legs are quite thin.
Was there oil on the bread?   Yes.   There she is.
I am on the sand.   Now I eat.

It's cooler in the gallery
but that love-girl was paler that I thought she'd be
like the gentle pastel air she displaces with her blond hair
and her modesty as Aphrodite arriving from the curly sea.

Taller too   almost life size   mounting the waves
behind the indifferent head of a uniformed attendant.   His shoes
are small and finely black as he bends and points his pointed
    toes.
Botticelli.   Her toes are bare as she stands in her shell
with a loop of hair to cover the pubic bone   carelessly held
fastidious fingers.   Now that I think of it they are pointing too.
A very knowing slender wrist: *Ecco la galleria*.
And the rest? Faded or fading away. Like the scent of the sea
    from you
still on my hands as we drift in bed under the roof   drowning
in light like watered silk from green shutters at the height of the
    day.

Were these clear things really there at the time?
I did not say them on postcards to myself.   But this
is a snap of us on the Campo. A fountain is in the background.
You can hardly see it. A pigeon is drinking from the throat of a
    wolf.

Out of Ward 6

Why did I not see it before?

The amazing shirt numbs the fingers
with its rough threads and packed checks
and the stiffness of the collar and the stress
of a tweed jacket tacked at the back
pipe the arms to rest at my side.

I never knew how trousers clutch
in the middle this way   to seize my thighs
like a randy cat and my soft feet
feel high and tight and wide   bound
to be weather proof   shut   in shoes

which will walk me away from here
squeaking and springing and light at the knees
out of the Ward and down the stairs
—which were always there but never seen
in a week of warm air and loose

pyjamas: (an even dream
that shut all texture out and
stopped time with ease   or turned it
round to counting nights and not
days   of nothing   doing   much.)

The stairs are different too and the air
outside   pares my cheek like a blue
razorblade   and touches me all over
to show I'm here still   still here
(almost) all of me here   so new

19

so strange   like the neat bricks
stacked at the gate going out. Wherever
did they come from? Dusty
visitors   arrived too late and I
never saw them before   or

their hard hard   veracious   edges?
Beyond the gate they are already
becoming more ordinary   even affable.
I think that we did meet
in another life   a week ago today

for a while.   We are just clay.

Family Group

Remote in boots and heavy suit
John Watson sits   with his beard
          his spouse   and his sons
ranked on the granite steps
of his house with iron railings
that rise to the door
like spears.   (A maid peers
through the window behind him.)

Great Grandmama Davidson
in black bombasine
               composed
wears buttons like an insect's eyes
and a look like the back of her hand;
before she came to visit
the curtains were washed
the children were pressed.

Uncle Alec   the bantam of a man
with spotted tie and flyaway collar
          the dandy grocer
stands stiff and feels his spurs
dreams of a spell in the Guards
packed between breeches and helmet
bridles there like a horse
—eighteen hands high.

Uncertainly   with a large hat
my father's father leans at the back
        a pale boy in a man's suit
he looks to the lens with my face.
I think of the photographer
all wrapped in darkness;   remember
to breathe again.
And leave them to it.

MacDiarmid at the End of the World
(for Mairi Anna Birkeland)

He stands where stones meet only stones now
where old boulders of porphyritic granite
seamed and crystalline   are wedged straight
and patched and speckled with moss and yellow lichen.
He wears a grey suit and a collarless shirt.
He has one foot set fast in the cold dyke
                    rising to Crowdieknowe.

Behind an overcast sky that glowers at odds
with a piercing diffusion of light and mackerel cloud
the straw-gold sun gathers and radiates
its life   as fierce and thin as hydrogen
pouring down on the rigid broken ground
more pure and accurate than the long unsaid
                    last word of God

until among the tousled graves the dead are up
and sprinting for the border.   They scale the dyke
to clamber back to the furious world.   He waits
with the other foot planted in bog cotton
milkwort   harebell   tormentil.
As they pass he tells their names.   Now
things really begin.   Thyme. Stonecrop. And Grieve
                    alone at the gate.

In the Fall Woods

Around us here your clear
nature   comes down
on me like sweet summer
rain   sweet summer rain
and the trees growing in the wood
turned into flame   turned
into flame   brought by our care
to autumn in a single day.

We went for a walk where
rain met   old leaves
scaling bark   grey lichen
moss   roots   and open stumps
rotting with cup-held pools
of cold fresh water.   October
pearls   misty in your hair.

I went for a walk around your eyes
and returning   saw something
burning there   something burning
some thing burning away . . . .

Surface Tensions

1.

In his bath he whispers a word to the steam
to himself   again and again: 'Girl.
'Girl.   Girl.   Girl.   Girlish.'
He can wait for her because she waits for him
(she waits for the boy in a magazine)
paper thighs   with jewelled hands on
silver skin   – naughty fingers in –
a glossy promise as sleek and blue
as a fish in the brown stream. He
thinks he knows what it must be like.
(A dream.) Not like loneliness.

2.

Or like these married two   who collide
found and lost and found again
driven on the swell of their own wave
to make love and leap and leap
and leap to meet the instant when
he rises like a salmon   hanging
on the blue air   – and breathes there –
only to drop down to the curdled pools
to be lost in the moss and the mud again
to face the journey one more time.
She rests   and counts how much it costs
to drown this loneliness.

3.

The managing Director knows how
much   as he tightens the straps
that bring him to his longing's wheel.
He racks the buckles till his breath
squeaks   so thin   so pure   so
sweetly bound;   and thus confined
his mind too catches just a glimpse
of blue   before the wheel trips
and the narrow lade thunders back
around his ears   and the millpond
opens out so calm   so still
in a daze beyond. (Mayflies flicker
under the sun and water boatmen
skitter sideways over tangled weeds
fathoms down   old iron
and slime below.) An hour passes.
He begins again to dream of the blue.
He thinks he knows what it must mean.
The word was loneliness   after all.

Sycamore Leaf for Celia

The leaf was   uniquely
worn   frail   faded.
One   pale shaded
side   surprising blue
and the other torn   between
grey drying veins.

It is oxidation.
It has other names.

In your bare hand   the leaf
was uniquely worn.
I found another   half green
and laid it there
lightly.   Your cool palm.
That evening.   Gathering games.

Londonderry Wall Love Poem: Certainties

Such sober certainty of waking bliss
I never heard till now.
        Milton, *Comus.*

Move into the light.   In a passion
of the moment I understood it   promised it
forgave it: 'To know everything   to see
everything right   to have it out for the best
without hypocrisy   without equivocation.'

When the News got back   it left me
prancing and talking   like de Bergerac
talking and prancing without rest
in the sooty beams of a bombed out
Belfast pub;   and the finger on certainty's
trigger zeroed-in again: 'Sure
you'd think they'd know enough to stay away'
– caressing the spring   squeezing death
like a skinny girl with her hand on her nipple
honestly   with a cold and tender elation.

Reflexions

After the first yell of shock   at the change
represented by a sewing needle through the finger
(new information)   there was curiously little pain.

   But the loved flesh is pierced with ease
   know it now:
   your loved flesh is pierced with ease.

   Bone might snap like blackboard chalk
   you stole at school   sing it:
   bones snap like that.

   And a bubble of air stops the heart
   though you will never hear it
   the   (pop)   that kills the heart.

After the first yell of shock   at the change
represented by a sewing needle through the finger
(new information)   there was curiously little pain.

   Iodine.

Poem

With my hand on your belly to feel the bairn
kicking through
      I was astonished:

to feel the stirring of my sex
and old Adam looking up:

to find beyond all act of love or friction
in such a careless one   a care for reproduction:

that I should be moved to the first act
by the rippling of the curtain:

that I should have raised such a cairn
with you   in the wilderness of creation.

Short Stories

1.   Eve

On accoont o luve at the beginnin, God Himsel
cam doon til Adam sleipan on a green bank his lane,
an wi ae stroke o His maist omnipotent han
drew-oot the leman Eve fae his runkled side,
juist as he pu'ed-in the warl wi its unco fish
fae aa that kirn o starns, wunds, an feck o angels,
tae set it like a braw stane i the ring o the heavens.

Sae Eve set fit on the banks o the gairden
wi the stag an the rabbit sae gleg,
wi the hoodie craw in the aipple-tree
an Adam aye sleipan.

Whiles she lookit at the craiturs i the field
loupan i the fresh-cut hay o Eden
an syne begood to kaim her gowden hair.
– An wi ae stroke o the tortoiseshell
she ruggit the haill warl back
til a sottar o souchan and pechan an preenan
wi feck o divils in ilka beastie's hert.
An the braw warl, wi its fish an its timmer
(an that guid gerss) she hung like a buckie
i the swell o her briests. (Aye, a buckie!)
Aa on accoont o luve at the beginnin.

(Or that's hoo the Faither telt it.)

2.   *Dido*

'Aye, Dido, I mind her. . .'

Cam then Prince Aeneas til Carthage toun
wi ram-beakit boats an a host o Trojan men
in mail coats and saut-weet gear tae be unloadit
on the strand. That year fowk said that the pikes o his
band o gleds were mair nor the trees i the toun hill.
The Trojans were fair taen wi the steir i the streets: seein
new waas biggit an prices risin near as fast,
an rare-laid cooncil plans for a haill city o trade, an couthie
speeches on dividends i the drouthie banquets o Carthage.

But Dido brunt for the Prince's luve. Brunt like a brand.
An nae rowth o siller nor hert's blae stang
brocht Aeneas back tae lie wi her an rule
her profitable toun. Ach . . . sae it was aa foretelt
by Venus i the wood that the bit Prince met on the first day
(the limmer wi her bow an her whippets, amd her arra pints
baith lang and sherp that win-in sae slee.) An him
sae canny, that wantit tae gang til Italy an bigg a city
for himsel (the trig rule o Rome – a stey gate)
an aye the canny yin, wi his plans for stanks an his fly
sheepskin sark, he was never really prickit in-by the hert.

'Aye, Dido, I mind her fine.'

3.   *Troilus*

A bit houghmagandie was aa it was.
(Troy was an awfu place for that
aabody kent it, it was even expeckit,
tho nae by the Greeks at the city waas
—a gey conventional crood the Greeks.)
Pandar never thocht she'd faa
(but she did) til the chairms o Troilus,
an sune they were snug in his ain box bed:

> *Come live with me and be my love*
> *And we will all the pleasures prove*
> *That hills and valleys, dale and field*
> *And all the craggy mountains yield.*

– Troilus on tap o Cresseid i the dark
(narra pairts thon box beds)
an aa was auncient sunlicht and cheer
as warm as maut and as pure as Plato
(she thocht). What he thocht was 'Hey ho!'

A bit politics was aa it was
that took Calchas til the Greeks
(that was the lassie's faither). Politics
is the chancy thing for diplomats
an necromancers. But kennan the future
like he says, he's nae suner by the gates
than he speirs for his dochter tae jine him.
Ye micht jalouse he could really see
the waas dung doun at the end o the tale,
or Achilles' triumph in his gowden cairt
wi michty Hector pleitered in the sharn,
and mebbe he could. Bonny Cresseid

jined her da. An eftir a whilie
she met a Greek (a hero cheil
cried Diomede), and he didna look
sae bad til her, sae braw in his pride
as he was – an on the winnin side.

A bit hertsair was aa it was
at first, but cocky Troilus fand
that it got waur the mair Cresseid
was gane. ('Ach, houghmagandie!'
says Pandar.) But Troilus saw her yet
sae trig and sure as a siller birk
that's pit doun seed i the mool o his hert
and wi its roots has happit his hert,
an ruggit awa an crackit his hert
wi thrang, naitural, surprisin dool.
– See Cresseid in Diomede's tent
(chancy airts thon airmy tents)
syne see Troilus his lane on the waas.
He wisna wyce tae faa for luve.
Did he no ken there was a war aye on?
Weel, he was mindit o't sune eneuch
by the edge o a sword at his lug in a barney.

See the Gods haen a canny lauch
at the trauchles o aa their bairnies.

On the Sea Rim
(Vancouver Island)

On the sea rim doun by the wrack
an leavins o the swell trailan
its timmer an kelp i the souch
o the saut ream, there cam til me
een the grace o your caller limbs
movan amang thae raw ferlies.

Syne on that sherp an winter strand
my hert gied a wrench like the roost's
faa til the toom shores o the warl,
an I was at your hand aince mair, lass,
for aa the watter's depth an wecht
atween us, an the gey distance
that is in it by land.

. . . reflections . . .

Mirrored
(for Norman MacCaig, 1910-1996)

Somewhere in Scotland by a hill loch
a man stands plain in his bones and casts
one (wary) fly   on the face of everything.

Here the world is (balanced) between
bog cotton   peat   and water-colour
water the colour of a dog's eye:

until every nameless colour of the place
shifts   – tree   bones   and the wary sky –
and the cold water stirs and the hook

tugs at the mouth of the hill in the loch
(in the fine corner of the plain man's eye)
and he plays it: the rod and the line

– Loch Culag   Glencanisp   Suilven –
bring back the shy world
note by note   to the dusk.

The Daily Life of Statues
(for Les Murray, photographed standing on a block of stone)

Pedestals must learn to be ironic
in an age of concrete.   And pillars too
from Corinthian acanthus through
Ionian volute to homely stumps of Doric.

Also pillars of the community   like that clan
of stately bronze persons who man (yes: man)
the city squares in Glasgow Paisley and Dundee
Coats Tannahill Burns Scott Watt and Livingstone

who stand through the long night-watches that
they share with deathless generals
– like mounted Wellington guarding GOMA
in his postmodern traffic-cone pokey hat.

Then there are upsets
like Manzoni's massive block of bronze
with the title-plate upside down
to signify a plinth under the earth

thus turning us   entirely around
falling upwards   off the ground
into an asteroid belt of cars   books
shoes   library tickets   parking tickets.

And sometimes they are empty   as here
inviting completion
with a quick jump onto the tier
and a properly ironic imperial pose.

But not everyone can hold them down
(the plinths of the earth) with such style
as he who came to Culross town
where there might have been Murrays

to re-establish a dream of kinship
and tell of new centres on the other side
of our perilous wordy worthy sphere
down under   inside this   over here.

Few statues   ponder   so well
and no bronzes manage such sprawl
(with the density of Saturn's hoops
in a jersey's many-coloured rings)

yet here he is   in the pause and power
of the moment on a veritable pillar
to say it's words and not the stone
which raise lasting columns of their own

nor any inscription
that's not re-cast with each new dawn –
all the way from   *a rare ear our aery Yaweh*
to   *me shivers and falls down.*

Trahison des Poètes
(for George Steiner)

> *'Think of it'* (he said) *'the unread inheritance of time;*
> *the billions of books – eaten by mice!'*

In stack after stack   down the line
of the word the little emendators go:
the scurrying   the squeaking   the signs
of incisive and democratic activity
(such close attention to the text).   Fine
shreds   mouse droppings   learned confetti
drift down from the galleries of Alexandria
to lime our shoulders with a cultured dust.

Ah my friend   *lektor*   *lecteur*   you must
get your teeth into that   if you can:
gnaw the text down to the bone.   Or hollow
it out   drill some holes
                and lead them away with a tune.

All the Time
(a recipe for William Carlos Williams)

The down on your neck in the light
of the kitchen
      window
            shining –

one glance as I passed the neat
room   – forgotten
      until now.
            (Separate

the eggs and whisk the white
together
      with fresh
            milk;

cold water over a gentle heat
stirring
      all the
            time.)

Where was I going?
And why in such a hurry?
      Cold water over gentle heat.
            Stirring.

A Chinese Moment by the Duckpond

Mandarins pose
on the edge of the pond.
With their smooth blue pates
and golden whiskers they plan
a ruffled elaboration
of ceremonial dress: stripes
collars and upturned orange fans.

One of them (quite overcome
by the occasion) lets down
his little pink feet
to paddle in the crystal stream.
His eyes are black yet
neat and madly fixed
like tiny beads of sewn-on jet.

Hardly noticed
on the dun bank
a lady rests among the group.
She is bare and brown
and content to be   there:
watched but not watched
by intellectuals at court.

Above it all   below it all
fish swim in the thoughtful depths.
They know where they are going.
They know nothing of gravity.
Or paddling. Or feathers.
'Flow is everything,' they say 'everything
is flow. And next to that comes scale.'

They are pure gold. All gold.
Golden voyagers in a world beyond
the dreams of the mandarin.
Perhaps there is a message here
or a meaning we should know.
The ducks.   The fish.   The golden air.
Shallowness.   Depth.   Flow.

Sunday Morning Evolution Lesson Poem

Outside   the dinosaurs are singing in the trees
or perched on the gutters they sit in pairs
and bend their bony knees
backwards   in the damp Sunday morning air.
          (The papers are late today.)

Inside   my books are arranged in rows
like old fossils filed with their backs to me.
Here time drips   it does not flow
and the line sticks   as it tries to be
          different.

How did the dinosaurs sing
and hop their way out of the immeasurable rock?
Surely it must have been a very difficult thing
for them to do? Why did their armour plating not work
          any more?

They make it seem so easy   bird brained
and content to claim their territory
by whistling for it: the same old refrains
piped over and over and over again
          the only oratory

that has survived one hundred and eighty million years.
Meanwhile   time drips and I'm losing track
among the books   with my daughter in tears
at the door 'Mend the quack! Mend the quack!'
          she says . . . .

And so I begin to bring back the lost song
of a broken wooden duck
   (it pulls along on a string)
an unlucky dinosaur who hasn't quite made it yet
   from off the study floor.

Postcards Home

1. *Postcards*

(i)

They arrive after you.
After you're home.
Posted far away.
Messages from another day
sent by a different person
to the one you came back to.

(ii)

I'm in a pool of light
the pool on the desk
sitting here   with the books
and the screen slow
scrolling   among the leaves
by the pencils in a jar
—and there you are
in a sun-parlour   120 miles
away   and years ago
in a sun-top and a headsquare
leaning forward – no –
looking forward to the long
trip   that will take us here.
So. Can you tell?
Could you then? Send
a postcard ahead   now.
Don't look back.

(iii)

What the break was
and what it really meant
lies somewhere between
the ones you didn't write
and those you forgot to send

from that city to the east
with its canals and trams
all so distant now
at least until the photographs
come back.

(The week end.)

2. *The Crab in Springtime*

'Canker is a disease of plants. Cancer of animals.'
    – *A Portrait of the Artist as a Young Man*

Birds are flying-in from some other nation
(Africa) I suppose   fragile
skeins and lines on the air-mail paper-
thin envelope of space. (Sky high.)

Those snowdrops in a jar   gather
around a trace of verdigris in their veins
(annihilation by the window) I thought
and (blue shade) and (still life).

And it hangs there   like a tribal rug
on the wall in shadow at the end of the room
– metastatic growth – and its unseen shapes.
(Cut to the sound of horn and reed.)

Height   /   hard light   /   Blue in Green.

3. *Looking through the Glass*

'Casements'   she said   'wide . . .'
'It's a window'   I said with scorn
'and don't give me "faery lands forlorn"
'because it says Gateside'   said I.

'But the window-catch lies
'like a blue sphinx in the sky'
she said   'and see how the panes divide
'the fields;   and where do the walls meet
'and why should the roads hide so
'and what is that red spot in the woods?'

'I never heard of such latitudes'
I said   'except perhaps in books.
'But I'm sure'   I said   'it said Gateside
'despite the queer light   and the way it looks.'

4. *Brown Study*

To begin with a leaf from your tree
spotted black and pierced away
like a page when it's old and dry
and the lines are   'foxed'   is it?
You can read the tale in time
but it says the same as last year's
said. It is in the book of trees.
(A common theme in the tree of books.)

You stand four enigmatically brown
clay garden pots on the shelf
– a water-stained and dusty collection
of empty volumes without a word
to say   (as yet)   to the seeds
to come.   'Auriculas'   I ask
'Do they mean little ears?'
We should get a flower book.

But you just sit there
with your Paddington hat turned down
all around   and a wooden egg
on a thong. I can't see
your eyes at all and only the lobes
of your ears   jumping through
golden hoops among the cabbage roses
on the chintz settee.
        'It's all been said'
I think and   'untranslatable as always!'
Yet the freckles on your nose exactly
match my cinnamon-rust ruined leaf.
I'll have to look that colour up
and check its name. In the freckle book.

52

5. *Holiday Cottage*

Outside   clouds and hills and sea
and shores between   stream by
as if to simplify all that gravity
to a matter of ink falling slowly
into the finely laid paper
of the sky   and its tattered edge.

Inside,   there are envelopes and lace
pressed flowers and wallpaper roses
– like those Paisley shapes   so
desperately entwined in the scarf
you bind about your hair;   or
my letter there   with its lines
like black ferns and scratches
saying this and that   or this . . .

Interiors get complicated:
there was a mirror too   playing cards
unmatched willow china   puzzles
and a knotted handkerchief
left for something to remember
– before the sun gave way
to lamplight   spoons and glasses;
and the patterns of our faces
where cold space was   and
the fine web of steady coming night.

6. *From the Compartment*

I saw a white horse through the window
– wish a wish is what you do – so
(safe journey) I thought and (good
travelling). A chalk horse standing
by the line to the downs   quietly.

This scene is called 'Train Landscape'
(a plain translation)   and it must
have happened like this   but
very long ago   (can you
smell the moquette?)   in a past
of third-class compartments (to be

explained later). Mean-
while   lower the strap and lean
out. Wave to the horse as
we pass. In a glimpse as fast
as light   as pale as bone.

7. *Back in the Room Now*

The spiderplant and the clock
(is there time in the jungle?)
on the shelf where the cat sleeps
and the leaves drip   as the paint
peels   on the window frame.

The spiderplant and the clock
where the hands move   too
slowly to see   though
slow enough to feel
I guess   as the garden
waits in its own frame
beyond the pane of glass
in a dim roar   meaning

the traffic of air   yes
traffic of air
as it passes between spiderplant
clock   paper   and this
reluctant ink.

Lines for Scotland
If it wisnae for the weavers. . .

To tell it plain
like the rocks tell it
or the peat moss layered
in the original grain:
a rediscovered part
of the world's crowded heart.

The warp an the weft o't
is the fabric o ocht.
The web an the binding o't
an the shuttle o thocht.
The feet and the hauns o't
aa thegither wrocht.

The beam an the frame o't
tae hailness brocht.

Wavelengths . . .

Bla Bheinn

Like a door   between the sky drifting
and everywhere you are: shifting
yellow light; ridge after ridge
of cloud and scree-run falls;
sgurr and rock in bands of glare
and heavy shadow;   layer
on layer   rising up
from the corrie in different hues
of stone and splintered light;
where granophyre   gabbro   dolerite
(sharp as axeheads and cinders
balanced on a narrow shelf)
slowly unlock the steady route
between space   and our careful boots.
        When we stepped through
        the yellow haze
        we saw another shore.
        (Door upon door).

Skye Shore

. . . upon this rock I will build
my church; and the gates of Hell
shall not prevail against it.
                    Matthew 16:18.

Sitting on the sea shelf
in Skye . . . taking notes . . . .
The shore is old; time's dump
at the frayed border of things. The glacier
waits its return. Like the tide.
The castle wall has fallen back
to rubble of boulders and building blocks
all alike   and worn without distinction.
Seaweed grows on each one.

Yesterday   the radio said the Pope
was dead. But what has he
to do with me? Now
two people play with a kitten
on the beach. A delta jet
flew over this morning   very low
burning black smoke   (slowly)
with a noise like caves and a stone
rolling away   somewhere.

The rock here is almost made
round. Smooth gravel trickles
between my fingers. Ground
down. Ground down just
by being itself   for long enough.
Christopher splashes on the salt flats
'Look at me! Look at me!' Being he
after seven years. And jumps in rubber boots
from stone to stone sunk like skulls

to their eyebrows in the turf. Here
we all were   balanced
on an afternoon at the edge of the West
(the Isles of the Blest)   collecting
shells   building sand forts   thinking
about St Peter   old atom
bombers   wet cats. Slipping
on the open shore   while the world
tilts its precarious shelf   towards the sun.

Nature Study

The pond is in a daze   reflecting
clouds   where lilies grow
open to the sun and slowly shut
to a darkening   dwindling   sky.
Beyond that thin meniscus   there lie
the stars   roots and shapeless rubbish
in the slime. Messages pour down
on the turning lily flowers: radio
waves   Doppler shifts in light
an unseen sleet of cosmic rays   – time
and matter too –   sifting home
to its bed. Galaxies fry
with voices like a cricket scraping
(singing)   on the border of the night.

Photocopy

It is happiest with text.
But when the book slipped
it caught my hand   intricately
plotted in dark and grubby
wrinkles   worn   creased
folded and written over
like some ape's apprentice paw
in shirt sleeves (checked).

But every other thing above
the fishpond of that static eye
– me   you   the spaces
between us (those confusing
bits) and all the smells and voices
to be found in the book of the rest
of the moving world – it prints
and gives back   as black.

So this is a picture of a pool of ink
and the hand of a ghost writer
(in frayed cuffs) floating up
to the surface of things   bearing
his crumpled palm and a printed page.
Yes. It is happiest with text.
The rest is
          unreadable.

FM

(Christopher Grieve d. 9 September 1978.)

I think it is coming closer   your voice
your death   hearing that laugh again
last night in cheerful conversation
crossing over the airwaves:
      a distant station transmitting

magnetic tracks from three years back
– fine traceries that leave a breath
hanging   between speakers   and the click
of your teeth on the stem of your pipe
      in a pause of eerie fidelity.

Under your tender fingers   black
with black twist   a knife used to make
aromatic tobacco shavings sprout and curl
like young ferns   into the cup of your hand
      to be crushed there.

– The moment's meaning was lost
to the blind spool   recorded then
as silence only. But time's translation
sends it on: the truth of it now.
      Crossing over the airwaves.

Wavelengths

Hence in a season of calm weather
Though inland far we be
Our souls have sight of that immortal sea
Which brought us hither
Can in a moment travel thither,
And see the children sport upon the shore,
And hear the mighty waters rolling evermore.

'Intimations of Immortality'

Talking of time and thinking of Wordsworth   I notice
how the old man sat with his back to the engine
to wave goodbye to a boy on the platform   lost
in study of the track   who did not see when the train
pulled out   and when the old man waved farewell
(the spikes   bolts   ballast   clamps and wedges
that bear the rails away and tie us down).

Now he looks through himself in the window   drowned
in reflections   as houses and rocks and stones
and trees roll by to the swell of telephone wires
across his closing eyes. The lines are humming.
Their voices will get there before we do.
A fat girl in a football scarf switches
her transistor on. Now we are grounded in the present. . . .

It seems our signals do not die. Like radio
echoes   filling the sky with burning fortresses
American cries   circling in the ionosphere
above Schweinfurt after the bombers found home.

      Lucky Lola is all on fire / I can see
      for miles / so clear / so true
      keep off the air / so thin
      so blue / leaving
      Louisiana in the broad daylight
      fallings from us / oxygen / silence
      hard rain / vanishings
      too late to stop now
      Lo Lo Lo Lola
      eight miles / high

In time   like other things   the signal transfuses
or decays   as grasses dust the tarmac and air-force
huts corrode to red in Norfolk fields   shifting
to the whisper of sun-dried stems. Rose
Cherry   Iron   Flamingo   say: 'Rust
never sleeps.'   I think: 'Memory does.'
Yet still the isle is full of voices

that blow away on the electric wind   and
burning roses   cherry cola   rusting flamingos
the lost boys   spiral up towards the stars . . . .
More earthbound   she tunes the dial again
' . . . in a season of calm weather . . .'
Immortal words keep coming through.
They will get there before we do.

. Go, Johnny go! Go!
Go Johnny, go! Go!
Go, go Johnny go . . . go.
Johnny B. Goode.

Fragments of radio transmissions have been picked up some time after their first broadcasting, caught in reflections between the ground and the Heavyside Layer. Ultra high frequency wavelengths, as used for television, are carried beyond the earth itself. On its own slower way out of the Solar System, the Voyager space-craft takes along 'The Sounds of Earth', a gold-plated LP disk which includes a song by Chuck Berry and instructions on how to build a record player.

This poem carries its own echoes, too.

Shades
Three elegies

They hae cam frae the skuggie airts.
Sydney Goodsir Smith, *Under the Eildon Tree.*

1. *Hugh MacDiarmid*

And stood in a burst o' sun
Glowerin' at the bit broken grun'.
– 'Ode to All Rebels'

If the thousand-headed heather were to start piping
in the wind on the slopes above Brownsbank   then you
would not hear it: and I might cry at the tunes under
the hills and you would point to the edge of the peat bog
to delicate   scattered   broken shells   (far from the sea)
– crumbs on the hungry rim of the water's brown mouth
which brings every living thing in time to the throat
of this old   soft   acid   land   – and you
would crouch by those calcined shards in the glaur and say
'Rain on the ocean's bed'   and   'The Pleiades'   and I would see
your mottled lips with the imprint of your pipe   move
and guess at the words   and the beautiful connections
but it would be all   without hearing them fall.

2. *Sydney Goodsir Smith*

Aa this will happen aa again.
Monie and mony a time again.
             – 'Orpheus'

I remember when the electricity failed
in an ersatz cellar-bar on Darnaway Street
and you read by candlelight and one eye
glazed   over the sole flame in a winter's gloom:
and we found ourselves in the narrow lands of Lucky
Spence and mad Monboddo   listening to a voice
like a worn saddle well-used with a careful stitch
here and there   discreetly creaking to a poem
about Spring in the Botanical Gardens: which took us
higher still to cold Dunbar on his windy ridge
chastising the speugs on the slates as plump as feathered
tennis-balls   cheeping the first notes of an old song
the riddle-me-ree of a cripple's wife who will not let us
rest for love   or decency or wit   nor age nor pity
nor a thin fog in the lungs: frame within
frame within frame   I see it clearly looking back
until the candle spales you into another night
beyond our extinct tavern fire   with its glass-fibre
logs   china dogs   and a formica ingle-neuk.

3. *Robert Garioch*

> The piobaireachd comes til an end, gin we may cry it end,
> the grund naukit again, as tho it had aye been sae.
> – 'The Big Music'

The New Town will not touch your body   wrapped
round in a greenish jersey like a fisherman
up from Leith   unarrested   for a day
out on the street of the Princes   rolling past
Sir Wattie's spire and maybe looking up
with a wary eye for doos: you dander
through the squares like a small   ironic
(greenish) cloud   loitering at the counters
of Jenners   or drifting over the agendas
at Charlotte Square   to see how the Arts
are coming   ('nae thing's pruven   naething
pruvable')   until the whole determined maze
of terraces and crescents   banks and schools and
offices and churches quarried in rectilinear
intransigent slabs   blows through you
like the stray scent from a clock of flowers
without weight at last   or the power to quell.

Winding the Clock
(In memoriam David Murison)

I dreamt of joy last night
something to do with grasses seen
against the sky   making
little arches and how the trees
could do the same   like green
tunnels into the blue

and we laughed and I remembered you
and how you wanted no-one
at your funeral   determined in the end
that you would have   – none of us.

But there was still laughter at the dinner table
and after a while I said 'and here we are
sitting around having taken snuff
and all our eyes are   – watering –
and we're sitting here solemnly
pretending   it isn't happening'
– and of course that set us off again.

It was a good dream.
The tunnel of grass.
The tunnel of trees.
And the circle together
with laughter under the sky.
And David at the bottom of the stair
who fell while winding the clock
was somehow there too – though of course
he wasn't really any more.

It was all   I think I see now
about love in the end
and the blessing of laughter
among good friends
when usually it's pretty different
– at the top of the stairs   in the dark
alone with the clock   in the stroke of night.

Oh, I am two fools I know
For dreaming and for writing so,
In whining poetry.
All this at four minutes past five
on a Wednesday morning in February
early enough   still alive.

But the feeling persists of
somewhere an open door
and somewhere the possibility
of seeing it through.

The Slope
(for John Coltrane)

to start in the middle of the sentence   running down
the slope towards the incoherent rubble of the shore:
where I told how each scored surface keeps
its own record of the forces crossed on the journey
to bring it there   – names   signs   single
words   broken cries and whole lines
torn from different histories   – all going
the same way   – all tilted into the sea;

where we turned our faces to the sun as waves of light
marched down in concentric rings   ordered and neat
as the dykes that curve across the brae   to say
'You can live here. You can't stay'; where Christopher
found a shattered sprig of cast-iron   curled
like ivy around a name – it spelled *The Singer* –
so we hung it from the branches of an oak whose trunk
was bent by air   blowing for years on a single theme.

In a house on the hill towards the end of the day
my father stands with his back to the sky and a book
in his veined hand. I cannot see my mother's face
for she turns away to watch a little girl
rolling on the yellow grass towards the door
the tree   the shore   the sun. Joanna shrieks
and laughs at the power of the world to draw her down
to join the discrete things at the bottom of the slope.

And I think of those spearing   repeated   notes
that call from tiny wavering tracks and fill my room
with your lost presence: where the tenor swoops
and climbs its way beyond the edge of the phrase
tearing sheets of sound from the unfinished sentence
– and floating through –   down   down   down.
And down and down and down and down   and down
down and down   and down   and down and down

– until there's nothing left to say at all . . .

The Schools of Siena

1. *Crossing to Tuscany*

Watching the cars go by the Motor-Chef
– the white lights coming and the red lights
going away –   penetrated by my daughter's hair
falling into her sleepy seven-year old eyes
– penetrated by the instability of things. . . .

Teachers charted atoms at school   (like bricks
in a builder's yard baked with dust on Helen's eye
or weighted with trees and Wordsworth and all)
they never told us we were the sky: bricks   books
yard   school wall   – all riddled with light
or rocked on the airwaves passing through
without a pause –   like ripples from a stone
dropped into the throat of the first well. . . .

The motorway went to a place where Dante was
waiting at the top of a round and rugged hill
(everything so green)   'Ah yes'   he said
'It is like that   but later burns to umber
under the sun. It comes close to us that star's face.'

(So the symbols gather standing in the snow
I keep to the back of my mind   to make them out
and know them as my own   – like the children
in a white garden beside a thin snow tower
who wears a carrot for a nose and shares
a coal-black   ferocious   grin with both
of them   and me   and you.)

Now we are south and into August. On the terrace
above olive trees and fields of blackened sun flowers
ants ferry crumbs across the tiles; at our feet
they make a double chain as each one halts
to check its fellow before it starts again:
to and fro   to and fro   to and fro.
Electric lamps burn at night   memories   wired
to each gravestone outside the village walls.
Rain spots fall from a clear blue sky.

In the afternoon things stop. We try to sleep
through waves of heat and thunder   and lie apart
in bed   attentive to a cataleptic sky which talks
only to itself   in language of the purest force.
Heavier and heavier   we sweat and itch
in the shade of old rooms with massive thwarted beams.
We dream of reaching light and snow   but tender dust
drifts down to teach us after all   how we go.

2. *Towards the Sun*
(in the gallery)

Our Lady of the Cherries   applauds
the baby with his fists full of fruit.

Our Lady of the Sparrow   inclines
her narrow head to the cheerful bird.

Our Lady of the Milk   suckles
one abstracted   hungry   little god.

        Her eyes are as clear as scalded almonds.
        Her skin is virgin olive oil.
        Her face is as pure as the face of a cat.

I look at: thinness of gold leaf.
A small town burning on the hill beyond.
The weight of nothingness.   Those blue heavens.

3. *No. 1 Via d'Ingresso*

Black swifts pinwheel round the square
and fix us to the ground.   They never
stop weaving their nets in the air.

Yet we found them unexpectedly as if
parked in corners   dead birds
neat   specialised   stiff.

We threw those sleek bodies over the wall
– where rosemary grows in a sweet
haze   of turpentine and menthol

– where the quick electric lizards meet
and the ants sustain their endless chains
around the passion flower   around our feet.

4. *The Life*
(at the abbey of Monte Oliveto Maggiore)

Our brother   who is white as a blanket
gives us milk-white chocolate to eat
lays his tender and hairless hand
on my son's blond head   tenderly
as his lips make a kiss on the gift to say
his silent blessings on us all
who stand still for them. Cold   dry
sunlight   sifts from the cloister wall.
San Bernardino is mending broken pots
again   – a canny miracle barely
fixed on Signorelli's fresco of humble ghosts.

In the Chapel (two hundred years later)
baroque and fruity muscular forms
strain   and vault into empty air and
eternal   hemispherical   space. We stand there
and I think of the poor clay below
and the narrow brick road we walked
worn hollow by our hosts' bony feet.
I think of raw wooden stakes   nailed
by wires to the milky horizon   waiting
for tendril vines to rise and cling.

The early fields are veined with poppies
in the cool air. Once there was nothing
here. The lesson is still emptiness.

We take our blessings with us.

Beyond the Edge

I'm drawn to the moment on a blade when steel
fades out of self and into nothing, on a line
fine enough to defy even the gentlest touch.

There were seven chisels in my father's toolbox
laid top and tail about   like sardines
(or packed on their sides like bottles of wine)
yet each one different   suited and ground
to its own purpose   and buffed
to a misty mirror-finish on the flat.

Unused for years   they speak of when
preparation seemed all there was to do
and as important as the job itself
in the fight against encroaching dullness
with hands that shook on those clouded blades.
This was to be his last anthology of sharpness.

Each chisel was taken to the limit
honed on a strap   and then laid by
keen   to make even the dullest timber
flower   – some other day perhaps.
I took them home and use them now
– and now and then I sharpen one. Thinking

nothing cuts forever. Thinking
of a molecular discrimination so refined
that you would feel nothing should the finger
slip to bone   —beyond surprise
at how the blood has come to marry oil
on the cold black stone below.

So we work to carve shape from sense
trembling in the confusion of the wild woods
out there   —where my father went to live
altogether away from sharp edges.
With a toolbox ready for every single thing
but that which came to pass.

Slender Walker
(for Jo at 21)

I watched her go with careful steps
in her frame of delicate bone
as she walked today on cobbled streets
of honey-coloured stone.

The old causeway will still be there
in the town above the river
but water flows towards the sea
and the world is suddenly wider.

End-notes and echoes

Postcards Home

I'm intrigued by the idea of postcards as ephemeral and cryptic messages to ourselves and those we love. I often buy postcards of paintings when I come across them in galleries to send to friends on various occasions. Some of these postcard poems are haunted by specific paintings, or by remembered (or misremembered) details in them that have somehow invaded the text – along with a track from Miles Davis's *Kind of Blue*. They are not poems *about* the paintings.

(2) Christopher Glanville, 'Sky High'; Graham Arnold, 'Venus on the Sun'; Elizabeth Blackadder, 'Still Life with Flower Heads', Miles Davis, 'Blue in Green'.

(3) Marian Leven, 'Window View, Gateside'.

(4) Rory McEwen, 'London Leaf'; John Morley, 'Old Florists' Auriculas and Flowerpots'; Harry More-Gordon, 'Portrait of Domenica'.

(5) John Fewster, 'Sunset, Rona'; Sylvia von Hartman, 'The Knotted Handkerchief'.

(6) Eric Ravilious, 'Train Landscape, 1940'.

Wavelengths

Acknowledgment is made to Chuck Berry for the chorus to 'Johnny B. Goode', echoed at the end of this poem (lyrics and music Chuck Berry). Other echoes include words and titles from The Who (Pete Townshend); Emmylou Harris (Rodney Crowell); Bob Dylan; Van Morrison; The Kinks (Ray Davies); The Byrds (Clark, Crosby McGuinn); Neil Young; also Wordsworth; Ezra Pound; Shakespeare; J. M. Barrie.

Shades

3. Robert Garioch. Agendas at Charlotte Square: where the Scottish Arts Council used to have its offices.

The Schools of Siena

4. The Life. One of the more modest miracles associated with the life of St Bernardino was the ability to resurrect broken crockery.

Some other books published by **LUATH** PRESS

POETRY

Drink the Green Fairy
Brian Whittingham
ISBN 1 84282 020 6 PB £8.99

Tartan & Turban
Bashabi Fraser
ISBN 1 84282 044 3 PB £8.99

The Ruba'iyat of Omar Khayyam, in Scots
Rab Wilson
ISBN 1 84282 046 X PB £8.99

Talking with Tongues
Brian D. Finch
ISBN 1 84282 006 0 PB £8.99

Kate o Shanter's Tale and other poems [book]
Matthew Fitt
ISBN 1 84282 028 1 PB £6.99

Kate o Shanter's Tale and other poems [audio CD]
Matthew Fitt
ISBN 1 84282 043 5 PB £9.99

Bad Ass Raindrop
Kokumo Rocks
ISBN 1 84282 018 4 PB £6.99

Madame Fifi's Farewell and other poems
Gerry Cambridge
ISBN 1 84282 005 2 PB £8.99

Poems to be Read Aloud
introduced by Tom Atkinson
ISBN 0 946487 00 6 PB £5.00

Scots Poems to be Read Aloud
introduced by Stuart McHardy
ISBN 0 946487 81 2 PB £5.00

Picking Brambles
Des Dillon
ISBN 1 84282 021 4 PB £6.99

Sex, Death & Football
Alistair Findlay
ISBN 1 84282 022 2 PB £6.99

The Luath Burns Companion
John Cairney
ISBN 1 84282 000 1 PB £10.00

Immortal Memories: A Compilation of Toasts to the Memory of Burns as delivered at Burns Suppers, 1801-2001
John Cairney
ISBN 1 84282 009 5 HB £20.00

The Whisky Muse: Scotch whisky in poem & song
Robin Laing
ISBN 1 84282 041 9 PB £7.99

A Long Stride Shortens the Road
Donald Smith
ISBN 1 84282 073 7 PB £8.99

Burning Whins
Liz Niven
ISBN 1 84282 074 5 PB £8.99

FICTION

Torch
Lin Anderson
ISBN 1 84282 042 7 PB £9.99

Heartland
John MacKay
ISBN 1 84282 059 1 PB £9.99

The Blue Moon Book
Anne MacLeod
ISBN 1 84282 061 3 PB £9.99

The Glasgow Dragon
Des Dillon
ISBN 1 84282 056 7 PB £9.99

Driftnet
Lin Anderson
ISBN 1 84282 034 6 PB £9.99

The Fundamentals of New Caledonia
David Nicol
ISBN 1 84282 93 6 HB £16.99

Milk Treading
Nick Smith
ISBN 1 84282 037 0 PB £6.99

The Road Dance
John MacKay
ISBN 1 84282 024 9 PB £6.99

The Strange Case of RL Stevenson
Richard Woodhead
ISBN 0 946487 86 3 HB £16.99

But n Ben A-Go-Go
Matthew Fitt
ISBN 0 946487 82 0 HB £10.99
ISBN 1 84282 014 1 PB £6.99

The Bannockburn Years
William Scott
ISBN 0 946487 34 0 PB £7.95

Outlandish Affairs: An Anthology of Amorous Encounters
Edited and introduced by Evan Rosenthal and Amanda Robinson
ISBN 1 84282 055 9 PB £9.99

FOLKLORE

Scotland: Myth Legend & Folklore
Stuart McHardy
ISBN 0 946487 69 3 PB £7.99

The Supernatural Highlands
Francis Thompson
ISBN 0 946487 31 6 PB £8.99

Tall Tales from an Island
Peter Macnab
ISBN 0 946487 07 3 PB £8.99

Tales from the North Coast
Alan Temperley
ISBN 0 946487 18 9 PB £8.99

THE QUEST FOR

The Quest for Robert Louis Stevenson
John Cairney
ISBN 0 946487 87 1 HB £16.99

The Quest for the Nine Maidens
Stuart McHardy
ISBN 0 946487 66 9 HB £16.99

The Quest for the Original Horse Whisperers
Russell Lyon
ISBN 1 842820 020 6 HB £16.99

The Quest for the Celtic Key
Karen Ralls-MacLeod and Ian Robertson
ISBN 1 842820 031 1 PB £8.99

The Quest for Arthur
Stuart McHardy
ISBN 1 842820 12 5 HB £16.99

The Quest for Charles Rennie Mackintosh
John Cairney
ISBN 1 84282 058 3 HB £16.99

ON THE TRAIL OF

On the Trail of John Muir
Cherry Good
ISBN 0 946487 62 6 PB £7.99

On the Trail of Mary Queen of Scots
J. Keith Cheetham
ISBN 0 946487 50 2 PB £7.99

On the Trail of William Wallace
David R. Ross
ISBN 0 946487 47 2 PB £7.99

On the Trail of Robert Burns
John Cairney
ISBN 0 946487 51 0 PB £7.99

On the Trail of Bonnie Prince Charlie
David R. Ross
ISBN 0 946487 68 5 PB £7.99

On the Trail of Queen Victoria in the Highlands
Ian R. Mitchell
ISBN 0 946487 79 0 PB £7.99

On the Trail of Robert the Bruce
David R. Ross
ISBN 0 946487 52 9 PB £7.99

On the Trail of Robert Service
GW Lockhart
ISBN 0 946487 24 3 PB £7.99

LANGUAGE

Luath Scots Language Learner [Book]
L Colin Wilson
ISBN 0 946487 91 X PB £9.99

Luath Scots Language Learner [Double Audio CD Set]
L Colin Wilson
ISBN 1 84282 026 5 CD £16.99

WALK WITH LUATH

Mountain Days & Bothy Nights
Dave Brown and Ian Mitchell
ISBN 0 946487 15 4 PB £7.50

The Joy of Hillwalking
Ralph Storer
ISBN 1 84282 069 9 PB £7.50

Scotland's Mountains before the Mountaineers
Ian R. Mitchell
ISBN 0 946487 39 1 PB £9.99

Mountain Outlaw
Ian R. Mitchell
ISBN 1 84282 027 3 PB £6.50

NEW SCOTLAND

Some Assembly Required: behind the scenes at the rebirth of the Scottish Parliament
Andy Wightman
ISBN 0 946487 84 7 PB £7.99

Scotland - Land and Power the agenda for land reform
Andy Wightman
ISBN 0 946487 70 7 PB £5.00

Old Scotland New Scotland
Jeff Fallow
ISBN 0 946487 40 5 PB £6.99

Notes from the North Incorporating a Brief History of the Scots and the English
Emma Wood
ISBN 0 946487 46 4 PB £8.99

Scotlands of the Future: sustainability in a small nation
Edited by Eurig Scandrett
ISBN 1 84282 035 4 PB £7.99

Eurovision or American Dream? Britain, the Euro and the future of Europe
David Purdy
ISBN 1 84282 036 2 PB £3.99

HISTORY

Reportage Scotland: History in the Making
Louise Yeoman
ISBN 1 84282 051 6 PB £6.99

A Passion for Scotland
David R. Ross
ISBN 1 84282 019 2 PB £5.99

Scots in Canada
Jenni Calder
ISBN 1 84282 038 9 PB £7.99

Plaids & Bandanas: Highland Drover to Wild West Cowboy
Rob Gibson
ISBN 0 946487 88 X PB £7.99

NATURAL WORLD

The Hydro Boys: pioneers of renewable energy
Emma Wood
ISBN 1 84282 047 8 PB £8.99

Wild Scotland
James McCarthy
photographs by Laurie Campbell
ISBN 0 946487 37 5 PB £8.99

Wild Lives: Otters – On the Swirl of the Tide
Bridget MacCaskill
ISBN 0 946487 67 7 PB £9.99

Wild Lives: Foxes – The Blood is Wild
Bridget MacCaskill
ISBN 0 946487 71 5 PB £9.99

Scotland – Land & People: An Inhabited Solitude
James McCarthy
ISBN 0 946487 57 X PB £7.99

The Highland Geology Trail
John L Roberts
ISBN 0 946487 36 7 PB £5.99

Red Sky at Night
John Barrington
ISBN 0 946487 60 X PB £8.99

Listen to the Trees
Don MacCaskill
ISBN 0 946487 65 0 PB £9.99

BIOGRAPHY

The Last Lighthouse
Sharma Krauskopf
ISBN 0 946487 96 0 PB £7.99

Tobermory Teuchter
Peter Macnab
ISBN 0 946487 41 3 PB £7.99

Bare Feet & Tackety Boots
Archie Cameron
ISBN 0 946487 17 0 PB £7.95

Come Dungeons Dark
John Taylor Caldwell
ISBN 0 946487 19 7 PB £6.95

Luath Press Limited
committed to publishing well written books worth reading

LUATH PRESS takes its name from Robert Burns, whose little collie Luath (*Gael.*, swift or nimble) tripped up Jean Armour at a wedding and gave him the chance to speak to the woman who was to be his wife and the abiding love of his life. Burns called one of *The Twa Dogs* Luath after Cuchullin's hunting dog in *Ossian's Fingal*. Luath Press was established in 1981 in the heart of Burns country, and is now based a few steps up the road from Burns' first lodgings on Edinburgh's Royal Mile.

Luath offers you distinctive writing with a hint of unexpected pleasures.

Most bookshops in the UK, the US, Canada, Australia, New Zealand and parts of Europe either carry our books in stock or can order them for you. To order direct from us, please send a £sterling cheque, postal order, international money order or your credit card details (number, address of cardholder and expiry date) to us at the address below. Please add post and packing as follows: UK – £1.00 per delivery address; overseas surface mail – £2.50 per delivery address; overseas airmail – £3.50 for the first book to each delivery address, plus £1.00 for each additional book by airmail to the same address. If your order is a gift, we will happily enclose your card or message at no extra charge.

Luath Press Limited
543/2 Castlehill
The Royal Mile
Edinburgh EH1 2ND
Scotland
Telephone: 0131 225 4326 (24 hours)
Fax: 0131 225 4324
email: gavin.macdougall@luath.co.uk
Website: www.luath.co.uk